AFRIYIE IS MINE
The Cost and Crown of One "Foolish" Act of Obedience

Based on true events

Dr. Asantewaa Aboagye-MacCarthy

Copyright © 2025 by Asantewaa Aboagye-MacCarthy

All rights reserved, including the right to reproduce this book or portions thereof in any form whatsoever.
For permission requests, write to the author at the address below:
amaccarthy.author@gmail.com

All Scripture quotations are taken from the World English Bible. Public Domain.

This book is inspired by true events. All names of real individuals and entities mentioned in this book are used with explicit written permission from the respective persons and entities. The author acknowledges and appreciates their consent to be included in this work.
Some names and identifying details have been changed to protect the privacy of individuals. Any resemblance to actual persons, living or dead, is purely coincidental.

DEDICATION

To Afriyie

I don't have the words. May the God you have so faithfully served honor you. I am blessed to call you husband.

FOREWORD

Having walked alongside Pastor Mensah Afriyie as a covenant brother for over fifteen years and based on the role I played, by the grace of God, in the birth of his covenant relationship with Dr. Asantewaa which has necessitated the inspiration of this wonderful epoch, I can confidently affirm that indeed the steps of a good man are ordered by the Lord.

The Afriyie I knew hadn't shown any keen interest in any lady though there was a bit of pressure from friends, loved ones and family to settle down. He seemed not to be bothered with all the suggestions and recommendations from well-meaning friends. Was it that he hadn't met someone who impressed him? Was he looking for something specific? Or was God simply working behind the scenes, aligning his steps according to divine purpose? In the process I got married and knowing the kind of person he was, I chose him as one of my groomsmen.

As destiny would have it, when my wife took in with our first child, she spent some time with her parents due to proximity to her gynecologist. In this period, Afriyie and I lived together for nearly a year. It was during this period that he told me he'd eventually chanced on a damsel that was causing some bubbles to bubble within his belly. When I saw his seriousness and how vehement he was on the fact that I join him to seek the face of God, I knew that indeed there was something unusual about this person he had seen. Upon enquiry, he told me how his path crossed this divine damsel.

I began to pray and the Lord showed me a vision of him and this lady cooking together in my kitchen. Then the Lord said to me "As different ingredients are put together to form one great meal, so am I bringing this duo together to become one great force". I relayed the vision to my brother which happened to endorse the witness of the Holy Spirit on the inside.

Fast-forward, communication went on between this

duo until one day he told me he wanted to visit this damsel and make his intentions known to her. I remember I had travelled from Accra to Kumasi for a week-long program and had to drive on the Saturday to Cape Coast to accompany him on this special day. We set out on a four-hour journey with joy, high hopes and anticipation mostly because of how they were beginning to know each other. They had been communicating on the phone for almost a year.

The outcome of our journey that day was a shocker; an outright bounce and such a big no from this damsel that it gave him goose bumps. After all God had said? We had to return to Kumasi carrying the weight of that rejection for the next four hours. Honestly, from my perspective and looking at my temperament, if I were in his shoes I would have moved on but looking at what has happened over the years and maturing through life's experiences, I have come to realize that God deals with us differently based on our frame. For me, when I met my wife, I told her my intentions point blank after two months of communication and gave her a timeline to decide. When it delayed, I nearly told her to keep her answer to herself. That's how impatient I was in such matters.

Many sympathizers got bored and advised Afriyie to move on, but he seemed not perplexed although one could see he was quite emotional because this was the first damsel that possessed such power to make our brother fall in love. He didn't give up but continued to pursue his dream with all resilience.

Along the line, the Lord brought a massive financial harvest for my brother. His status changed suddenly. Perhaps now, things would turn in his favor and Asantewaa would reconsider. So, he approached her again only to be slapped with another bounce. He did a few things to prove his love for this damsel afterwards but none of those things moved her.

Well, life goes on. We live to fight on.

Three years passed. This brother, as much as he tried to move on, seemed to be back on a factory reset where no one caught his attention like this damsel did. A lot had happened in between with Asantewaa graduating as a valedictorian and continuing to do her internship.

Then this duo started talking again. I believe that

this was the perfect time the Lord had ordained.

In the visions of Asantewaa, an angel of the Lord brought a message indicating it was time she considered the proposal and not delay about it. This is because she had also spent time seeking the will of God on the matter again. Through prayer and counseling from some mentors the Lord gave her, the Lord brought her into alignment and ordered her steps back to His will. And this time, when Afriyie asked, she said yes. At last, the dream that had once seemed out of reach had materialized. Glory to God!

Few weeks down the line, the vision I had received came to life - the duo in my kitchen cooking rice balls and peanut butter soup. And now they are a strong couple that is getting married soon or even married already as you are reading this book. I believe you're already excited and yearning to know more, especially from this beautiful damsel.

This whole journey brought out a lot of valuable lessons I believe will be a blessing to you as the author takes us on a deeper dive into her experiences as she dared to obey God and apply his Word. It teaches us to trust God's will and timing for our lives. It teaches us the power of prayer, patience and resilience in our pursuit of the will of God. This book I believe will be a blessing to all singles as well as married couples and anyone seeking to pursue the will of God in any area of life. Stay inspired as we journey together through this wonderful book.

- **Pastor Charles Koomson**

Head Pastor

The Redeemed Christian Church of God – Powerhouse

Accra, Ghana

ACKNOWLEDGEMENTS

This section could be a whole book on its own. Many people have played key roles in ensuring that the purpose of God would prevail in my life. Some, I have met personally whereas others have impacted me strongly from afar.

Mama D, I love you so much. You have been the kindest and most loving mother. I know that it was hard for you to accept Afriyie as the man for me. I know that this difficulty stemmed from the heart of a mother who desires the best for her daughter. Despite your reservations, you humbled yourself and held my hand to accept the path God had cut out for me. You opened your heart to Afriyie and made him your son. You have done well! May your heart of love be preserved by God and may His mercies never cease in your life.

Pastor and Pastor Mrs. Koomson, my angels in

human form, I love you! When I felt tossed by the gruesome wind, you flooded my life with love and guided me with your counsel. Words fail me. I am immensely grateful. May God comfort many more hearts through you.

Dr. Jerome Abaka-Cann, less than a year with you and you left an indelible mark of love on my heart. Your counsel is a like a cool breeze on a scorching summer day, offering a welcome relief from the sweltering heat of uncertainty. Your humility is remarkable. The day I shared with you my journey with Afriyie, you shed tears. You cried with me and now, you will laugh with me. God bless you Sir.

Mount Zion Film Productions, do you know that your movies speak louder than tens of thousands of words? You have impacted so many lives and I am glad you chose Jesus. A million thanks fall short. God bless you!

Pastor Debola Deji-Kurunmi, you embody the strength of an unyielding oak, providing shelter and guidance to those who seek wisdom. You have planted seeds of wisdom that have blossomed into a deeper understanding and a more intentional way of living. Woman of valor, you are a great blessing to humanity.

Pastors JJ, KK, and BB, though I cannot acknowledge you by name, this section would not be complete without saying a huge "thank you" to you all for being generous with your lives and sharing it with billions. Thousands of miles from you, the impact reached me and changed my life. For submitting to God, thank you.

INTRODUCTION

One's choice of a marital partner is of extreme importance to God. Marriage is a huge deal and the person you choose to do it with can make or mar your life. For a child of the Kingdom of God, you have a divine mandate, the success of which affects not only you, but many destinies connected to yours. Many know this and so are wise to inquire of God's will concerning their marital destiny. What is difficult for most is yielding to that divine will of God. This is so because often, the will of God for us is far from the ideas we have about the perfect spouse. A conflict sparks between flesh and spirit. The battle rages on in our minds and unfortunately, the flesh wins in many cases.

It was difficult for me to yield. I tried to logically reason my way out of it. My flesh fought the will of God. Many times, I tried to escape the cup I had to drink, the death I had to die. For three years, I fought. My soul was troubled, and I cried, "Abba, why must mine be this way?"

Surrender occurred by the mercy of God. My divine strength, Who is the Holy Spirit, led me one day at a time to the place of surrender. I stopped fighting God and released my life into His loving Hands.

My heart cried, "Father, glorify Your Name!"

And He has glorified it in every way.

By the direction of the Holy Spirit, I wrote down the details of the journey to that glory. I present to you the heart of a loving Father who gently and patiently helped me to accept His offer of a man after His own heart.

And now, to the gist…

PROLOGUE

3ʳᵈ May 2023

Afriyie called me. I had not spoken to him in about three weeks. The past three weeks had been warfare. I had been fighting in the place of prayer. Actually, I had been fighting for almost three years, but the past three weeks had been a different kind of warfare. I saw the enemy in my dreams... the one who had been shooting arrows of confusion at me. I saw him face-to-face and fought him. I was riding a horse at top speed through a foggy path, but I was approaching the place of clarity. God had decreed my victory. That call from Afriyie was my victory.

He asked me how my day was going. We spoke calmly to each other...silently, we both knew that it was settled in Heaven. When we ended the call, I sat in my consulting room, feeling all funny. It was surreal to me because it had taken so long for me to find the peace I was feeling. I picked my phone and saw a message from him.

It read, "I love you, my girl. Be safe!"

I stared long at the message, looked up to Heaven and smiled. Ohhh the humor of God!

I replied, "I love you too, my man."

We couldn't say it on the call, but we were longing to. It was done and the One who did it is Jesus.

CHAPTER ONE: NOT MY TYPE

When the Holy Spirit told me to preach His Word on YouTube, I didn't know it was to position me to be found. I had finished a seven-day fast with my good friend, Jimmy, toward the starting of a Christian channel on YouTube. For months, the Holy Spirit kept hinting at it, so I discussed it with Jimmy and immediately, a seven-day fast was declared. To be honest, I had not considered it big enough to fast about it but when Jimmy brought it up, I embraced the idea and somewhere within me, I knew the Lord was up to something with this channel. Along the line, the Lord revealed to us what the name of the channel should be. The name, Goshen, became my prophetic name through that fast, and eventually, it became the name of the ministry God gave me. That fast yielded a lot of fruit.

23rd June 2020, I uploaded my first video. I wore a red top and my natural hair with some tendrils hanging on my forehead. I had no beautiful set for the video, no expensive equipment, no special lighting, and no makeup, nothing extraordinary. Just me sitting in front of my phone, facing an open window for some natural lighting, and speaking God's Word. I am stressing these facts to establish that there was nothing physically beautiful about me to appeal to the physical senses of a man.

The day after that post, I received a message from an old friend, Ben. He had shared my video on an online college alumni platform. He mentioned that a friend of his watched the video and wanted my phone number to say a few words of encouragement. I liked Ben; he was kind and very friendly, so out of courtesy, I gave him my consent.

That evening, I received a text filled with elaborate vocabulary, all to convey a simple message: "well done and keep it up". I appreciated the sender and there was nothing more. A few days later, that same individual texted me that he wanted us to speak on the phone. What about exactly? I didn't know.

Somewhere late June 2020, I got the first call from Afriyie. He sounded like a British royal with his extravagant choice of words. I rolled my eyes a few times at his polished diction and sophisticated language as we exchanged pleasantries and finally, he introduced himself as Pastor Mensah. He went on to applaud me for the work I had begun and praised me for my appearance which honestly came as a shock to me. He appreciated the modesty in my looks and encouraged me. It went somewhat like this:

Him: A blessed magnificent day to you lady of God.

Me: Hi, good afternoon.

Him: I have been anticipating this encounter and oh my, what a splendid day this is. I watched your video and initially, I didn't know what to expect but as I continued to listen to the message, I was like, "Wow, this lady is something else". God bless you for availing yourself to be a Deborah in your generation. In a world full of immorality, it was exhilarating to see you present yourself so modestly. Keep it up.

Me: Thank you

Him: By the way, my name is Pastor Mensah. When I

saw you, something moved within me and I said to myself, "Who is this lady?" So dear, tell me a bit about yourself.

Me: My name is Asantewaa. I'm a fifth-year Optometry student at the University of Cape Coast.

Him: Wow. That's wonderful. I'm seeing a lady who is very precious to God and her parents.

Me: Mmm yh.

Him: Have I zoomed into the prophetic? Haha.

Me: Haha, you are right actually...

It was a normal conversation to me but to him, it was so much more than just a few words spoken. I spoke to him casually; he spoke to me with intention. From the very beginning, he came in as a man who was interested in me as a woman he would want to settle down with. He didn't say it verbally, but I knew it. The issue was, I was absolutely not on the same page with him. I didn't know him, but I didn't like him at all.

The weeks passed and he kept calling. He shared God's Word with me, commented on my videos and gave me ideas for new videos. He also probed into my life. He chipped in questions like, "on a scale of one to ten, how neat are you?" "What food did you eat today and how did you prepare it?" He literally asked me to describe how I would prepare jollof rice. Hm. He wanted to know things I considered very unimportant when it came to marriage. It made me dislike him even more. More weeks passed and he got more comfortable with me while I grew queasier. He shared personal things with me which I listened to silently.

He was in a relationship with me, without my consent!

I didn't clarify my stance with him because of two reasons: first, my flesh and the pride in me told me to leave him to his fantasies. I found it strange and frankly, annoying that a man would just barge into my life like that and expect that I would simply like him back. I knew nothing more than his name and the part of the country he lived in. He never asked about my relationship status or whether I was interested in him too. He simply settled on me, comfortably made me his long-distance girlfriend and I had no part in it. Second, I had a knowing in my spirit that God was up to something bringing him my way. I didn't like that knowing. I fought it whenever it crossed my mind that this man could be…no, no, no! I didn't want to think about it. My eyes literally welled up whenever I saw the image the Lord had begun to paint. So, I chose not to talk about it.

Let's pause for a moment and talk about who I was at this time of my life. I was a Christian, a prayer plus fasting, evangelizing Christian. I loved God greatly and deep in my spirit, I wanted to please God in all things. The only bit about me that was off was the fact that I was too alive. Asantewaa was too alive. I still had my own future which I had created by my will, desires, and pride. To live was not Christ.

I met Afriyie at a time when he was the last type of man I wanted to marry. I didn't think much of him; I had not met him, but I had seen a picture of him and oh my, I didn't like what I saw. He wasn't the cool kind of man that I desired. My man was thick tall, godly but kind of bad boy. You know what I mean. Today, I look back and I wonder, "Who was this girl?" But that was me then.

Though I knew for certain that I did not like Afriyie as a woman likes a man, I knew also that he was greatly esteemed before God because the Holy Spirit bore witness to his purity and genuineness. I purposed to be polite to him, answer his calls every now and then, while I wait for my Mr. right, and probably, the Lord would settle him with another woman. Honestly, there were times I prayed for God to help him find a woman who would love him back.

Around that time, I chanced upon a video on YouTube where a Prophetess of God sent out a message to singles trusting God for good partners. She mentioned that in that season, she perceived that a lot of people would meet their partners, only that they would not immediately find them to fit into their desires but with friendship and conversations over time, they would find that these partners were God-sent.

That message made me cry. I knew God was speaking to me, but it was not easy for me to accept it. Why must it be this way for me? I cried. The Lord calmly asked me, "All your life, have I ever given you anything which fell short of best?" I knew the answer was no. God had been very gracious to me. I didn't grow up in perfect conditions, but I had the best people around me who loved me dearly. They were committed to ensuring that I lived to my fullest potential. So, the Lord was right. I had always received His best. Only that in this instance, I did not see what God was seeing.

Somewhere in October 2020, the Lord taught me something in very strange way about labels and substance and how many substances can be judged wrongly because of incorrect labelling. On October 6th, 2020, I wrote:

Can I borrow a thing or two from Solomon…I have seen a thing under the sun! Labels can be grossly incorrect…

I went to the clinic highly expectant of a busy day. I needed 20 cases to submit at the end of the semester and I was just a little past halfway to that goal. I sat down in one of the consulting rooms literally sulking over every minute that passed without a patient walking in. It was 11am already, an hour left for my shift to end. Then he walked in…

He handed over his clinic card with his folder ID and name written on it. I couldn't be happier. With the passing seconds in mind, I bolted to the records room and gave the card to the keeper. He began the search for his folder and that became another story.

Fifteen minutes passed and the folder still couldn't be traced. I joined in the search, combed every single consulting room, every drawer, and every space that could store something, searched among the records again and again and still nothing. 25 minutes had passed. My patient was getting impatient, and you know what? So was I, for crying out loud!!

So, I did what I knew to do. I prayed, "Father, please guide me to this folder, Amen."

The Holy Spirit led me to the records room once more, specifically to a table. Doubts ran through my mind. I had thoroughly searched through all the folders on this same table a couple of times already. So why was I being led back to it? I remember pondering over these. The Holy Spirit said to me:

"Up until now, you have been searching for a folder bearing the ID number written on the clinic card. What if that ID number was written wrongly on the patient's folder?"

As uncommon as that might be, it was a possibility. So, I changed my search method, this time using the name and further confirming it by the documented history in the folder. It didn't take a minute. I found his folder, and indeed, the ID number on the folder had been written as ***9, instead of ***1. The label was wrong, but the substance was exactly what I was looking for.

Within 30 minutes, God had taught me a lifelong lesson - labels can be wrong, hence, focus on the substance, not the label.

There are so many things and people we easily overlook and don't even give a single chance because their label doesn't fit what we may be looking for. But hey, labels can easily be changed or corrected. Substance, however, is substance...it is what it is. If we searched by substance (what people or things really are), we would find that so many of them have the wrong label.

Though I wrote this, and though the Lord had used a real-life situation to teach me this important lesson, I was still not having it when it came to Pastor Afriyie Mensah. He was simply not the kind of man I wanted to be with. So, I kept giving him the cold shoulder. Christmas came and another year was approaching. The night of 31st December 2020, the Lord gave me a set of instructions for the coming year. The topmost one was "Never run away from God". I wondered why the Lord would say that and why I would even want to run away from my own Father. He also gave me a Scripture,

'The sacrifices of God are a broken spirit. O God, you will not despise a broken and contrite heart.' (Psalms 51:17)

I didn't think too deeply about these. A new year was coming and that was all that mattered to me. 2021 came and I was expectant of a peaceful and beautiful year.

On the contrary, 2021 was a year of death.

CHAPTER TWO: HE WRESTLED WITH ME

Many times, we have interpreted the wrestling match between God and Jacob as Jacob wrestling with God and prevailing, which led to the Lord blessing him and changing his name to Israel. However, if we look carefully at the scriptures, we see that it was not Jacob who started the fight. He was left alone and then "wrestled with a man". Wherever the man came from, we do not know, but it is clear that Jacob did not go looking for a fight.

'Jacob was left alone, and wrestled with a man there until the breaking of the day. When he saw that he didn't prevail against him, the man touched the hollow of his thigh, and the hollow of Jacob's thigh was strained as he wrestled. The man said, "Let me go, for the day breaks." Jacob said, "I won't let you go unless you bless me." He said to him, "What is your name?" He said, "Jacob". He said, "Your name will no longer be called Jacob, but Israel; for you have fought with God and with men, and have prevailed." ' (Genesis 32:24-28)

Jacob had not lived a "good" life since his childhood. He was a son of promise, a grandson of the great man of God, Abraham. Though he came from such a man of obedience, the Lord had not had His way with Jacob. The Lord desired to bless him, to fulfil through him the promise made to Abraham, but the Jacob at that time had not yet aligned himself well with God to be blessed. So, the Lord fought him. This battle was not targeted at destruction but brokenness.

When God destabilized Jacob, it wasn't to hurt him but to humble him. God did all this to position Jacob in a place of surrender, a place where he would cry out for a blessing. God came down with the blessing in hand. In fact, the blessing was Jacob's right by the dictates of the covenant with Abraham. But God had to bring out a different Jacob from the old one who would deserve and attract the blessing.

In the year 2021, God wrestled with me. It was a year of a lot of sorrow but also a lot of growth. It had been about ten months since I met Afriyie and still, my stance was unchanged. We talked often. He talked with me as a man talks with a woman he loved and I, well, I was unmoved. April came and I turned 24. He and a very good friend of his, Pastor Charles, were coming to Cape Coast where I lived. They had been invited to a program, and decided to pass by to see me, for the first time, in person. I was unsure of how I felt about it.

At this point, I knew two things: first, I wanted nothing more than friendship between Afriyie and me. Second, he was a good man who truly loved the Lord and would make for a good brother in Christ. So, I decided to host them as a good Christian would.

3rd April 2021 was a sunny Saturday. My mum and I cleaned the house in anticipation for our guests and I prepared jollof rice with green chili pepper sauce and some chicken. I did not want to embarrass myself, so I prepared something I was very confident about. At about 3pm, Afriyie called me that they were almost at my house, and my heart skipped a beat. Why was my heart beating though? It's because deep down in me, I wished to also love this man back. He was kind and godly. I hoped to have a change of mind and maybe, seeing him in person and talking face-to-face would do it.

I walked out to meet them and Afriyie gave me a little hug. I smiled and did my very best to be pleasant. I greeted Pastor Charles whom I had spoken to a couple of times on the phone. Pastor Charles saw me as Afriyie's "beloved". In fact, all Afriyie's acquaintants knew me to be "the one" for their brother. The fact that it was not settled at all was known only to Afriyie and me. We sat down, exchanged pleasantries and Pastor Charles took leave of us to visit another friend. My mum gave Afriyie and me some space to chat. It was a very awkward conversation. He started,

"I was watching one of your videos with my friend and I said to him that this is the woman I want to spend my life with. And all this while, I have not said this over the phone because I wanted to give you the respect you deserve by saying it face-to-face."

Hm. I couldn't say much. All I said was "Thank you. I've heard you".

From there, my mood changed. This man was a good man, praised by God! But I was just not on the same page with him. There was a conflict within me. The Lord was saying something, but it was not what I wanted to hear. I could have simply told him that I wasn't interested, but I couldn't. I didn't want to offend God. For some reason, I thought God would not love me anymore if I outrightly rejected Afriyie. I was afraid and that fear made me unreasonable.

Indeed, I have come far in my understanding of God. Today, I look back and realize that I could have handled the situation much better if I had been mature enough in my understanding of God, marriage and people. I would have been honest with Afriyie from the get-go and asked for time to think and pray through it. I would have taken time to work on myself, confidently approaching God in prayer and seeking wisdom on the subject of marriage. Then, I would not have complicated matters and Afriyie would not have had to suffer through the mess. That day in my house was the ideal time to gather confidence and speak plainly to him. I could have reciprocated the same respect he gave me.

When Pastor Charles came back, he could sense the

change in my disposition. He was unhappy about it. I was unhappy about everything. We said goodbye and they left. I knew that I had made a very bad first impression. A man poured out his heart to me and all I could do was to be upset about it. I felt ashamed of myself. I felt inconsiderate and selfish. But sincerely, I couldn't help myself. I had hoped that our first encounter would help me like him but at the end of that encounter, I saw no hope. My mum asked me if I liked him as he liked me, and I shook my head. My mum didn't like him either. He didn't look like what we wanted. He didn't have the standing we wanted. We couldn't see what God was seeing.

From that time, I started to pray. I prayed for God to help me tell Afriyie that I saw no hope of a love relationship between us. Unrequited love hurts and I didn't want him to be in pain anymore. On the other side, I wanted the burden on my head lifted.

One day in May, God answered my prayer. It was a warm afternoon, and my heart was heavy. My phone rang and it was him. I said a silent prayer before picking the call. The usual warm voice of Afriyie was absent. He didn't say hello.

He simply asked me, "if I wanted us to be in a relationship toward marriage, what would you say?"

No more innuendos or faint signals...just straightforward. The moment had come.

I replied, "I would say no. I am not interested in a relationship with you".

Maybe Afriyie will tell his side of the story one day. I don't know exactly what happened to him at that moment. There was silence and then he said "wow".

I now know that I should have kept quiet, but I kept talking on and on about how I didn't think we fitted each other and how I had been waiting to vocally turn him down since he was not picking the signals I was sending. Afriyie was quiet.

At the end of my speech, he said, "wow, woooow, well, it's not a crime for you to not like me back. I understand". We ended the call, and I thought the storm had passed. I breathed a sigh of relief and said thanks to God. The Holy Spirit asked me, "are you happy now?" That question was the beginning of my death.

I was not happy. Though I had said what I had been

wanting to say, I was not happy at all. I felt empty. The Holy Spirit had been with me for a while, and I had learned to pick up signals of His disposition towards certain things. He was quiet within me, and I felt far from Him. That evening, I couldn't pray. I entered the Throne Room with my head down. What was wrong with me? I didn't have that joy I always experienced when I prayed. Afriyie didn't text me or say anything in any other way to me that evening. I slept hoping for a better tomorrow.

The next morning was a bitter pill. I woke up to texts which broke my heart. He had sent me many messages... scattered messages without any particular order of reasoning. I got scared. He expressed disappointment, and then a bit of anger mixed with many emojis and just so many things. I was expecting some form of reaction, but this was beyond anything I anticipated. The Holy Spirit told me to call him which I did. The first time, he didn't pick up. I didn't know what was happening to him...his messages painted a picture of a very distraught person. Now I was worried. So, I called again, and he picked up.

My heart sank at his voice. It was mingled with tears and pain. He sniffed when he spoke indicating that he was crying. I didn't have anything meaningful to say. I simply asked how he was doing, and he quietly said, "I'm not okay".

The days following that conversation were very bleak. Guilt weighed so heavily on my heart that I sank into depression. Each morning, I woke up to a text from him. Random thoughts on how he felt and questions on why I led him on.

"But I didn't lead you on!!!" I yelled in my mind. "I never told you or anyone that I was interested in you!!! You led yourself on and I (the truth hit me here) ...well I... I should have said something. I should have helped you instead of just watching on."

I knew this man loved me. All his friends had heard of me. His family knew me. But I pretended to not know. I didn't treat him as a person deserves to be treated. I didn't think much of his feelings, and I spoke arrogantly and cruelly to him. I felt he should have settled the matter with me before deciding one-sidedly that we were meant for each other, but my attitude was inexcusable.

When pride, ignorance and fear join forces, you

know it's going to be messy. I was full of pride and thought little of Afriyie's heart. I had very little knowledge of how to handle such situations where a man expresses interest, and you don't feel the same way. And I was afraid that if I rejected Afriyie, a good and godly man, God would hate me. What a mess!

That season was one of brokenness. It started with deep remorse. Honestly, I felt really sorry for how I had treated him since I met him. I realized that a lot of hurt could have been avoided if I had just offered him a little guidance.

"Hey, I have realized that you are looking for more than just friendship, but I am not ready for that" or "I know you like me, I appreciate you, but I do not feel the same way" or something around those lines at an earlier time would have helped him to limit his expectations.

I wanted to go back in time and do things right. Each morning, I woke up to a text from him...random thoughts. They expressed pain, regret, and a broken heart. I dreaded those messages to the point that I hated waking up.

I didn't know he had fallen in love with me. So,

when I insensitively turned him down after almost a year of saying nothing, I didn't know that I broke his heart into a million chunks. And now when I think of the fact that I hurt a man like Afriyie, my heart breaks.

He tried to be strong, but the first stage of grief was obvious; He was angry at me. We stopped talking for some time, he stopped commenting on my videos and posts, my guilt wouldn't let up so I tried reaching out to him to explain myself and try to be his friend again, but he always gave me the cold shoulder. I knew he was trying to protect his heart...nobody wants to be bitten twice.

At that time, I had my own share of grief. I felt so guilty and condemned that praying was difficult. When I met people, unconsciously, I wondered if they had also hurt someone and if they hadn't, how fortunate they were. I envied them. I compared myself to strangers, people laughing on the street, and I wanted to be them. I just didn't want to be me, the wicked, selfish, and inconsiderate girl. These thoughts filled my mind continuously. I was going crazy. I agreed with the devil when he condemned me. At this point, it was a full-blown guilt attack, and I couldn't break free.

On August 14th, 2021, I expressed how I felt in writing. I wrote:

> A few years ago, a friend offended me. I remember being so upset and I felt so wronged that for days, we stayed apart from each other. I stayed away because of anger and disappointment, but my friend stayed away because of shame. He could not lift his head to look at me because truly he acknowledged his fault. A couple of days after, with all the courage he could gather, he approached me and genuinely apologized. I nodded and said, "it's fine". But it wasn't fine. Because if I really meant it, I would not have spent the following weeks always reminding him of what he did. I held his mistake over his head. Whenever he was about moving past it, I brought it up. I stifled him. I enjoyed seeing him squirm because deep down, I was still upset. He was drowning in the pool of his own regrets and I, his friend, would give him no space to breathe.
>
> Fast forward to 2021, I also offended a friend. And I must say that it does not feel good to be stuck in that pool. I also apologized sincerely to my friend. And honestly, all I wanted to hear was "it's fine, let's just move past this". I apologized again and again and wished for things to return to normal. I felt so

weighed down by guilt…my fault haunted me for months.

Truly, I regretted what I did, and my biggest wish was for my friend to see that and forgive me. I remembered the incident years before and suddenly, I wanted to go back, hug my friend, and revive his soul…just help take that burden off.

I believe only God Almighty knows the true state of a man's heart. When we offend someone and are remorseful, He sees it because He is All-knowing. But sometimes it is not enough that God knows the truth. We want men to also see our hearts and forgive us. Many times, all people can do is to say sorry and hope that they'll be forgiven by those they've hurt.

Slouched shoulders, head down, Apostle Paul before the remaining disciples repeatedly saying sorry, just hoping that they would see his heart and forgive him for his past errors against the Church.

The tears are known to God alone for men cannot see beyond what they want to see.

I've been offended and I've been an offender. I know that at times it is really hard to let it go. But for the sake of those who are drowning in the pool of genuine remorse, please forgive and let them in for a hug.

Then I had a dream. I was sitting with a man in his fifties. A lady I knew came to us and showed the man all the mistakes I had made in an assignment she gave me. She was loud and mean. She pointed to all my mistakes in a book and demanded punishment for me. The man calmly defended me, to my surprise, and told me to pray so that I can identify the attacks of the enemy and rise above them.

That dream had me in tears. For the first time in a while, I prayed with my head lifted to Heaven. I thanked the Lord for His visitation and sought His forgiveness. His instruction to not run away from Him now made sense. I had been running away from God because I felt too sinful.

I proceeded to call Afriyie. I was back with the Holy Spirit and He was moving my heart to call my Afriyie. Thankfully, he picked my call. I cried like a child. I said sorry uncountable times and I meant it with all my heart. With a very soft voice, he told me to stop breaking his heart with my tears *(Dear reader, is there anyone more romantic than Afriyie?)*. He accepted my apology and changed the conversation.

I knew two things here: First, Afriyie truly loved me

as a man loves a woman, and second, I felt something, but it wasn't the kind he was looking for.

God had broken my pride and now, I approached my friendship with Afriyie with an open heart. But I didn't love him like a woman loves a man. I didn't feel what he felt. The Lord had started to wrestle my will, but it wasn't broken yet.

CHAPTER THREE: I SOUGHT FOR WISDOM

The bitterness of the past season awakened a hunger in me for knowledge. Ignorance had to be conquered. I was a very good student and excelled very much in my academics, but truth be told, I was quite ignorant when it came to the subject of dating and marriage. I had never devoted time to studying the Scriptures and other godly literature for the mind of God concerning this area of life. I knew I wanted to marry at some point, but the immediate past experience had taught me that there was a lot to learn. Therefore, I humbled myself at the feet of the Holy Spirit in prayer and cried out for wisdom. As I prayed, the Lord led me to Proverbs 12:4. It read,

"A worthy woman is the crown of her husband, but a disgraceful wife is as rottenness in his bones."

The Holy Spirit took the word "crown" and broke it down. He taught me that a crown qualifies the king. A crown is set on the head of a king and is in full display. There must be agreement between the head of the king and the crown, in that, the crown cannot be too big or too small, too heavy or too light for the head it is going to sit on. The crown must be the perfect shape, and of the right material. What was the Lord teaching me here? Compatibility!

I learnt that marriage is the joining of two like substances, forming a covalent bond where each partner contributes to the destiny of the other. There is a core being to each person and by the wisdom of God, He finds individuals whose core beings are compatible and joins them for the fulfilment of His divine mandate. The personalities may be different, likes and dislikes may be different, but there is a fundamental being which blends effortlessly with that of one's God-given partner. There is a common mandate which marital partners should not struggle to identify with, and to be able to discern who a suitable partner is, one must first know who they are and what God created them for. This brought us to the very vital issue of purpose. Without having a conviction of what your purpose is, you will not have any conviction concerning your life partner.

Before these lessons, I remember once acting like Gideon and asking the Lord for a sign concerning Afriyie. It was a Saturday morning, and I was washing clothes with my mum. I asked the Lord to move my mum to ask me about Afriyie and I would take that as a sign that he is my God-given husband. I was so anxious throughout that morning because deep down, I was afraid that my mum would ask me about Afriyie, and I would have to accept that he was my husband. I intentionally diverted our conversations to topics far away from marriage and anything that could bring up Afriyie. I had asked for a sign, but I was manipulating stuff.

I cannot help but laugh at my foolishness when I think about it. We finished washing and there was no talk of my man. I breathed a sigh of relief. That evening, I went to God with a strong position. According to that morning's test, Afriyie was not the one for me and if that was the case, then I was going to take him out of my mind and concentrate on developing myself as a woman of substance. I made an agreement with God that if I focused on personal development without trying to find a man for myself, the Lord would bring my husband to me when He knew that I was ready for marriage.

The thing is, God did not give me that sign at that time, not because Afriyie was not right for me, but because God knew that I wasn't ready to receive that information. I would have cried if that test had been positive. I would have obeyed God maybe, but without any conviction of my own that my husband was right for me. I would have felt like being thrown into a dark ocean by my "inconsiderate" Father in Heaven who cares nothing for what I feel.

By His mercies, God helps us to come to the place of acceptance of His perfect will, that is, if we allow Him to help us. I was not yet at that place. I didn't even know my purpose. I had not yet surrendered my will. The process had begun but was not yet complete.

I stayed true to my side of the agreement and committed to personal development. The Lord took advantage of that to refine me in many ways. I spoke to Afriyie sometimes, just a hi here and there for the sake of peace. I graduated as valedictorian and became a doctor.

I took up leadership roles and put myself out there. I studied the Scriptures so vigorously, prayed intensely and intentionally, and simply focused on God and me. It was a period of steep spiritual growth for me. I encountered gentlemen who expressed interest in me, but I had closed that door for a season. All I wanted to do was learn.

I started to read books on marriage and relationships. There was an insatiable hunger for more knowledge. As I read, I realized the flaws in my mindset which had caused me to make many mistakes in the past. I wished I had known all that before I met Afriyie. I definitely would have handled the situation better.

Afriyie reached out intermittently, brought up the issue of marriage again and again but the answer was still no. I must have said no about eight times over the three years we knew each other before I said the word he wanted to hear. Each time, he took the bullet, withdrew a bit and showed up once again with the same intention.

Progressively, I got better at rejecting him. It was no longer a stone-cold, "I'm not interested in you" but a more intelligent and thoughtful answer which either way still meant no. I explained why I was not interested in a relationship at that moment and how I was pursuing personal growth. I had purposed to treat him kindly and by the help of God, I got better at it.

Somewhere in the middle of 2022, Afriyie and his wonderful friend, Prophet Gideon, visited Cape Coast and passed by my house. Once again, he came with an intention. The night before their visit, I spoke at length with Prophet Gideon who encouraged me to accept Afriyie's proposal. He praised his friend so much and assured me of Afriyie's unwavering affection for me. I took it all in, thanked him, and fell at the feet of Jesus in prayer.

Deep within me, I wanted to follow God's path. Afriyie wasn't what I desired but if the Lord willed it, I wanted to follow that will. I prayed deep into the night, asking the Lord for His guidance. I went as far as saying,

"Lord, take absolute control of my heart and tongue. Let me say the words You want me to say. Move me in the direction of Your perfect will".

That night, I was highly expectant of a dream which would help me make the right decision but none of the dreams I had that night was about Afriyie.

The next evening, my visitors came home. I was very anxious. I gave Afriyie a little hug immediately he got down from the car as an expression of friendship and lack of any animosity. I was happy to see them. My mum put on a smile and welcomed them. In the middle of our conversation, the issue of marriage came up which turned my mum's smile upside down.

I knew my mum didn't like the idea of Afriyie and me together. I didn't like it either, but that day, my mum's stance on the matter was made clear. She expressed, unequivocally, her disapproval to anything which looked like marriage between Afriyie and me. I understood her to an extent.

My mum had raised me singlehandedly for the greater part of my life. In her eyes, I was the most beautiful and gifted woman on earth, and she expected nothing less than a king/sophisticated professional/beautiful man with impeccable grace to marry me. I knew what she wanted and Afriyie wasn't it. That second visit was worse than the first. Honestly, I felt sorry for Afriyie.

That evening, the two future love birds sat side-by-side to talk. I spoke to him from the standpoint of compassion. I hated that he was going through such pain and disgrace. I didn't feel what he felt for me and my greatest desire at that time was for him to love and be loved back. I told him to live his life and forget about any prospect of marriage with me.

But he didn't or more accurately, couldn't. To date, both of us cannot fully explain why Afriyie could not break free from me. He went through heart break and countless rejections, yet his conviction remained and his love for me never dwindled. I see it as divine enablement. It went way beyond anything physical; there was a divine force at work, ensuring the fulfilment of God's perfect will. Today, I honor that resilience. As for me, the Lord had a lot more work to do on my heart. Afriyie retreated from me but only for a season.

At this time, I had graduated from school and was doing my one-year mandatory internship. I had already planned out my life – it was internship, then out of the country to pursue a PhD and then...marriage? I had already begun applying for PhD positions because I was certain that it was God's will for me to enter the world of academia. I just didn't know how marriage fitted into the picture the Lord was painting.

We have unnecessary worries, don't we? If we believe that God is holding the brush, then why do we have worries? Worrying makes us fret which causes us to make hasty decisions and destructive mistakes. I worried quite a bit about this because I am a woman, and the path cut out for me was unconventional. The Lord had led me into a six-year professional doctorate program and right after that, He was leading me into a five-year PhD program. "When will I marry?" I asked Him. Rather than giving me an answer, He simply told me to trust and obey. So, a PhD it was then.

Strangely though, The Holy Spirit kept pressing on the need for me to prepare adequately toward marriage. My busy schedule didn't allow me to read on the subject as much as I wanted to and that was when by the leading of God, I discovered a lady Pastor who was well versed in the topic of marriage. To protect her privacy, let's call her Pastor JJ.

I remembered vaguely seeing some pictures of her, usually in the form of thumbnails on YouTube but I had never listened to any of her messages. Somewhere late 2022, I listened to one of her messages and I was hooked. I downloaded many of her messages and listened to them whenever I closed from work and was walking home. A few weeks later, I came across a video where Pastor JJ and her husband preached side-by-side on a vital marital issue. I was doubly hooked. I listened to them whenever I had the chance and gradually, my understanding of marriage was deepening.

One of the turning points of my life was after I listened to the testimony of Pastor JJ on how God led her to her husband. I call it a turning point because that message made me desire so strongly, the perfect will of God for my marriage. I knew I wanted God to guide me to the right person, but it had never been so strong of a desire.

As I listened to this woman, my mindset was undergoing a major shift. I identified so much with her experiences leading to marriage. She had to let go of her idea of a perfect man to make room for God's perfect will which at that time had none of the qualities she desired.

Whenever I listened to her testimony (and I listened so many times), I inched closer to a place called "surrender". I started to pray with tears which I couldn't control. There was a conflict in my spirit. If I was going to obey God, I knew I needed The Holy Spirit's help. Each time I prayed, I asked for the grace of obedience.

June 2022, I was having a conversation with two of my friends, Dr. Naa Adjeley Addo and Dr. Regina Antwi, when I came across a picture of a couple on Facebook. Something struck me about them, and I passed my phone to my friends to admire such a beautiful couple. It turned out they were Christian movie actors based in Nigeria. One conversation led to another, and Mount Zion Film Productions, a Christian drama and evangelistic ministry based in Nigeria, became a topic. Naa Adjeley and Regina educated me excitedly about movies and skits produced by the ministry and how God was using them greatly to win souls and reach His people. When I heard movies and God in the same sentence, I didn't need to hear more.

You know, God knows us so well and knows exactly how to get us in the right place, with the right information and people, all for the sake of His glory. So here I was, discovering for the first time what would later become my favorite things to watch on YouTube. Naa Adjeley recommended that I watch a movie called "The Train" to get me started. My excitement was through the roof.

Where was this excitement coming from? From the Holy Spirit within me who knew that He had me exactly where He wanted me. I sat down with the Holy Spirit, said a little prayer about how I wanted the Lord to speak to me through the movie, and started watching. Two hours, forty-four minutes later, I had entered through the first gate of a realm called brokenness.

The sounds in the movie made me sad within my spirit. They were chants which I didn't understand but they moved me so much. The aura in my room changed and I fell on my knees weeping with so much sorrow in my spirit. I wept so loud that for a while, I couldn't hear my mum knocking on the main door. She had been calling my name, but I couldn't hear her. When I opened the door, she was so disturbed. It was her first time hearing me sob so loudly and passionately. For days, she kept asking why I was crying. It was hard for her to believe that I was crying that way in prayer.

The movie, "The Train", made me see the cost and crown of obedience. Deep in my heart, I wanted what God wanted but I found it so difficult to simply obey God in the matter of my marriage. Even though the Lord had not told me expressly that Afriyie was His perfect will for me in marriage, I knew it. No matter how hard I tried to shut it out, it still stood against my efforts. In those few moments of prayer after watching the movie, my spirit called out to God to help me obey Him. I looked at the lead character, and I wanted to be him.

"The Train" was the beginning of the Lord's work in my life through Mount Zion Film Productions. I watched their life-changing movies which equipped me with knowledge and understanding. It was a refreshing season. The Lord led me to a movie titled "The Ignition" which played out the story of a young man whom the Lord had so graciously gifted a beautiful woman to help push him through life. This young man, however, rejected the woman at some point because of her health issues (she had epilepsy) which he considered embarrassing. In the end, he deviated into a rocky marriage which the Lord had not ordained. His God-given helpmeet was given to another man who recognized her worth and helped her overcome the disease in prayer. The young man was left empty without his helper.

Once again, this movie brought me to my knees. I could hear God so clearly. Never had I met a man as interested in and supportive of my gifts and destiny as Afriyie. Yet, a few things about him which I didn't consider so appealing made me reject him. I could hear God speaking so clearly! So, I fell on my knees and once again, cried out to God. I asked the Lord to help me accept the gift He was giving me in Afriyie. I asked God to help me see what He saw in him. I asked God to help me surrender to His perfect will.

But nothing happened immediately. I still didn't have any inclination to contact him or discuss marriage with him. For weeks, I simply kept praying. Around that time, I met many young men who expressed interest in settling down with me. All of them were fully devoted to God, in active service to God, and faithful warriors of the kingdom who deemed me fit to do life with them. I was pleased that these were the types of men I was attracting. God was giving me options. Handsome options.

But somewhere within my spirit, I knew what the perfect design looked like.

I became more intentional about praying about my marriage. I asked God for nothing short of His perfect will and if that was Afriyie, then, may He help me to accept it.

Afriyie had stopped speaking to me for some time. The Lord had begun to bless him financially and he was doing well. I was happy for him and praised God for lifting His son. Somewhere late 2022, Afriyie travelled to Nigeria for a Church conference. I don't know what happened to him at that conference, but he reached out to me once again with the intention to marry me. Though I had a little conviction that the Lord wanted me with Afriyie, it was a weak conviction, and I was also undergoing a major transition in my life. It was around the end of my mandatory internship and though I had applied for PhD positions in the US, I was not sure of where and who I would be in the next year. I didn't consider that transition period a good time to make a marital decision.

Most importantly, I was still in the process of discovering my purpose and I had learnt from Pastor JJ and her husband that one's single years are for identifying one's purpose and beginning on the path of destiny. They taught that everything one needs in life to fulfil destiny is found on the path of purpose. I took that advice quite personally and sought the Face of God concerning the purpose for which He created me. I knew that if I sought first the Kingdom of God, everything the Lord deemed necessary to my fulfilling destiny would be added, and that included the right life partner.

I remembered the agreement I made with the Lord that I would be focused on personal growth and making the best of everything He gave me, and in His time, He would lead my husband to me when He the Lord knew that my husband had become essential to that season of my life. So, humbly and very sincerely, I recorded a voice note to Afriyie, explaining why I was not interested in marriage at that time. I clarified that it wasn't because he was not good enough but because I perceived that it wasn't the right season.

At this time of my life, I had a few young men around me who had also expressed interest in me. I gave them all the same answer. Frankly, it was easy to turn down some of these men because within my spirit, I knew they were not it. Without making any conscious assessment of them, I simply knew to say no.

The thing about Afriyie was that the Spirit of God within me was drawn to him. Though I turned him down severally, I couldn't get him completely out of my mind. Anytime I imagined my married life, unintentionally, I made him the male lead character. I was changing from the lady who saw Afriyie as a "no no no" to one who saw the priceless heart he had, his calm demeanor and meekness, and the faintest possibility that one day, I'd bear his name. Even so, I said nothing to him and simply moved on with my life. He also withdrew from me and this time around, for months.

In the latter part of 2022, I had a strange dream where I had cut off my own head. I was very much alive and active, but I was headless. In the dream, my mum saw me headless and got very worried, but I told her that I did it to myself and assured her I would be fine. But deep inside, I was regretting what I had done. I saw many people around me in the dream, one of whom was Afriyie.

It was a very disturbing dream. When I woke up, I prayed seriously about it and asked the Lord to help me. I understood the dream because the Lord used a language He and I understood. "Head" meant husband. I prayed for the Lord's mercy and asked for grace to not deviate from the perfect plan of God concerning my marriage.

I continued my studies on marriage. I listened to Pastor JJ on the regular. I didn't know when I would marry but the Holy Spirit impressed on me to prepare for it. 2022 ended and I entered 2023 on the note of praise. That 31st December night, the Holy Spirit instructed me to praise God. I didn't ask for much concerning the coming year. I worshiped the Lord and thanked Him for 2022.

CHAPTER FOUR: 2023

The year 2023 had a rocky start but the Lord is ever faithful. On the tenth of January, I made an unexpected move to the Western region of Ghana to work. It was impromptu and undesired because I had to leave my mum, and it was emotionally difficult for both of us. But the Lord had a plan for me.

I began at the main branch of Imperial Eye Care Center where I met our CEO, Dr. Jerome Abaka-Cann for the very first time. I had spoken to him severally on the phone but had never met him in person. The warm environment at the clinic made it very easy for me to settle in and make friends. Within a week, I had adjusted to my new setting and my mum was also doing very well. The Lord helped us to adjust quickly because He separated us for a very good reason which at that time, we didn't know.

Fortunately, my boss came to drop his kids at a nursery which was in the same building as my apartment, thus, I got a ride to work every morning. That 10-minute drive from the nursery to the clinic became a strategic time for God to speak to me. My boss was a very devout Christian, filled with wisdom from God. A few conversations with him here and there and I realized that in him was a rich tapestry of godly knowledge. Each morning was simply wonderful.

On 8th February, I was interviewed for a PhD position at a university in the US. That same day was Afriyie's birthday and so I called him. It had been a long time since we spoke on phone. As usual, he was kind, calm and collected. I sang a birthday song for him and prayed with him. It was as though two old close friends had met at a reunion...we communicated so easily. I was happy to have called him.

Sometime after that, the Holy Spirit taught me the importance of honoring one's helpers. We had studied the friendship between King Solomon and King Hiram of Tyre. Though Hiram was of great help to Solomon, Solomon did not appreciate Hiram as well as he should have (1 Kings

9:11-14). With this lesson, the Holy Spirit instructed me to send messages of appreciation to key helpers in my life. I sent one to Pastor Afriyie Mensah because he had been a blessing to me and my family. That evening, he replied with a jovial message on how I'm his girl for eternity. He mentioned that he would love for us to talk whenever I had the time.

In early March, I had a dream where a messenger came to inform me that I was losing my husband to another woman. I saw Afriyie with a woman standing by his side. When I woke up, a part of me was a bit worried because I wondered why the messenger referred to Afriyie as my husband. Was it my mind playing some tricks or something? Anyway, the greater part of me was happy.

I was happy because Afriyie would finally be free of me and find peace and joy with someone else. It was a very selfless happiness I was feeling. But again, what if that was a merciful warning from God? If Afriyie was the perfect will of God for me, then losing him to another woman was a disaster I couldn't afford. I had learnt a thing or two about the extreme importance of purpose and locating the Kingdom path and I knew that having a God-ordained partner was vital to fulfilling one's purpose. So, I took my prayers up a notch and poured my heart out to God. I needed help to align with the perfect will of God for me.

On the 23rd of March 2023, I had a dream where I saw myself and four other people standing side-by-side, holding hands, and praying. To my left was a man I did not recognize. To my right was Pastor Afriyie Mensah, to Pastor Mensah's right was his very good friend and brother, Pastor Charles Koomson, and to Pastor Charles' right was his wife, Mrs. Ethel Zoe Koomson.

I woke up slightly disturbed. The Holy Spirit drew my attention to the order of arrangement and how we stood holding hands as one. I prayed to God for clarity. "Who was the man to my left?" I asked. To this day, I cannot recall what he looked like, but I just knew that someone was there. "Why was Pastor Afriyie to my right?" I asked the Lord. "How does my destiny connect to the Koomsons?" My mind was full of questions. I prayed for understanding.

On the evening of that same day, I received an admission offer to study for a PhD in vision science in the US. I was overwhelmed with joy. Now, I was certain of what was next for me in life - more of school.

But then, why was I being drawn to Afriyie and marriage? "If school was next, then how does marriage come in?" I pondered. As a woman, the experience would be quite different if I was to start my PhD journey and marry while in school. What if I got pregnant? How would I balance family life and school? Would my husband be supportive? What if he's not? Questions upon questions! I wanted to figure everything out.

The next day, March 24th, I had a strong desire to call Afriyie. He had already indicated that he wanted us to talk and catch up as old friends, but I wanted to discuss something deeper with him. Was I the only one getting these dreams? I wanted to know. So that evening, as I sat on my bed with my phone in hand, I looked up to Heaven and prayed, "Lord, please take control of this conversation. Help me, please". And I called him.

For the very time in our conversations, I did the questioning. There was so much I wanted to know. I asked him why he was so sure that I was the right partner for him. He answered saying that from the very first day he saw me, he had a strong knowing in his spirit and the Holy Spirit gave him peace concerning what he was perceiving. I asked him if he had inquired of God concerning my purpose on earth and how he fitted into that purpose. I got no answer for that. I asked him to describe who I had been revealed to him to be. I got no answer. So, I made a request of him to pray concerning the questions I had asked him. I also asked him if he had gotten any dreams or leads which indicated the kind of role he was to play in my life. There are many reasons for encountering people and I wanted to know if he was brought into my life to be anything else other than my husband. At the end of the conversation, we both decided to pray concerning this matter so that we would be on the same page.

I asked Afriyie some difficult questions that day. Those questions reflected my confusion and dilemma. After we talked, I was a bit tensed. I didn't want to give him hope and then crush it later. I didn't want a repetition of what had happened before. I prayed even more and asked for grace.

In that season, I had an attack of confusion which felt like I was carrying a very heavy weight. Whenever

CHAPTER FOUR: 2023

I woke up in the morning, thoughts flooded my mind and just when I felt that I was getting some clarity, everything got jumbled up again. I perceived that the Lord had something in mind for Afriyie and me but whenever I wanted to follow that knowing and take some steps towards it, concerns about the differences in who we were and what we wanted to pursue flooded my mind and stifled my intentions.

Afriyie was 33 years old at that time and was ready to settle down. I was 26 and had just gotten a PhD offer which would require that I leave the country. I couldn't merge the two lives without seeing conflict and chaos. I just didn't understand why God was leading me to a man who was so different from who I was. I tried to figure it out and create a meaningful plan, but my head could not contain it.

I was sinking in confusion. I prayed to God for help because I didn't want my jitteriness to mess up God's plan. I was afraid and burdened.

One morning, while going to work with my boss, I discerned that I should seek counsel from my boss concerning the matter. He was a man of the Spirit and had experience with marriage. That morning, Dr. Abaka-Cann gave me an advice which led me to the secret place. He gave me a prayer assignment to inquire of God of the type of man He wanted me with. Did God want me to be a Pastor's wife and help my husband in fulltime ministry? If so, then how did the academic bit come in? My path was an unconventional one which required an idiosyncratic approach. Only God could give me the wisdom I needed.

The Koomsons

The 10th of April 2023 was Easter Monday. I left Cape Coast for Takoradi to resume work after the Easter break. Throughout the trip, my mind was full. I felt a heavy load on my head which would just not go away. Whenever I tried to think, my head got heavy and so many voices filled my mind. Before me were so many paths and I didn't know which one to take. Immediately I got to my room, I fell on my knees and cried out for help. I needed direction because honestly, I felt lost.

That evening, thoughts flooded my head; one image here, and another there…the confusion was hurting me, and I knew it was an attack from the enemy. I prayed for help and confessed the scriptures. I wished to speak to someone, but I felt that no one would understand me. I knew my mum did not like Afriyie very much and so I didn't know how to tell her that I felt led to him. I needed an unbiased counsel.

Then, Pastor Charles Koomson called me. Afriyie had informed me a few days before that Pastor Charles wanted to speak to me. So, the morning of April 10, I had called him, but we couldn't speak for long because he was busy. When Pastor Charles called me, I didn't know what to expect. It had been a long time since we spoke. He began speaking with a very sympathetic and fatherly tone. He mentioned that Afriyie had spoken to him concerning the questions I asked him and how I suddenly brought up that topic. It seemed that Afriyie was also quite confused about those sudden developments and sought guidance from the Koomsons. The moment Pastor Charles started speaking, I knew that help had come. He said the words I wanted to hear so badly:

"When Afriyie spoke to me concerning this situation, I felt sympathy for you, and I understood what you were going through. You are a young lady at a very crucial junction of your life, and you are expected to make such a life-changing decision. I understand that it's not very easy for you".

I felt a rush of wholesome love. For about an hour, he edified my spirit with good counsel, shared his own experiences with me and helped me to see a shade clearer, the kind of picture God was painting with my life.

After that first conversation, I felt lighter and wanted to call Afriyie, but the Holy Spirit restrained me. I didn't know why. I called my mum rather to say goodnight to her. We had a normal conversation and somewhere in the middle, she narrated a chat she had had with someone who needed some form of direction in life and how she advised the person to pray. When she said, "so I advised him to seek the face of God concerning the matter. I advised him to pray, just pray and let God handle the rest", I heard it as though she was speaking directly to me. I heard, "pray, just pray". I perceived a call to prayer.

But I had been praying all this while! I had been praying since the beginning, so what other type of prayer was I supposed to make? I was a bit confused.

Around 9:30pm, I received another call from Pastor Charles. It was a conference call including his wife, Mrs. Ethel Koomson and Pastor Afriyie Mensah. It felt like an intervention. Mrs. Koomson began to speak, and I felt doubly loved. Afriyie left the call at some point to give us some privacy so that I could express myself honestly. Pastor Charles spoke few words throughout the conversation, allowing the two ladies to talk. We spoke for hours. She shared her crossroads experience with me where she was also torn between two men, not knowing the way to take. She encouraged me to not be anxious about how God would merge my marriage, academics, career and ministry. He is God after all.

In that conversation, I realized that I had been trying to be God. I wanted to figure everything out and be certain of all things before taking a step. That trait made me overthink all the time. When she spoke, I felt like I was staring at myself in a mirror which revealed all the hidden faults in my way of thinking.

Then she asked me a very important question. She asked what my conviction was concerning Pastor Afriyie. Aside from the dreams I had had and the feeling I could not explain, did I have any conviction concerning this man or was I just dwelling on a gut feeling which was subject to manipulation? I told her that it was just a feeling. She then gave me a prayer assignment to draw a conviction from the secret place which would become the foundation of the decision I would make concerning Afriyie. Only when I am fully convinced that he is my marriage partner or not would I break free from the manipulating thoughts of the enemy. I would no longer be dilly dally about this issue and drag it forever, but I would be certain, bold and firm in my ways. I would make a decision based on what I knew to be the truth, and no one would be able to take that from me. And lastly, she added "God will orchestrate His purpose into fulfilment". After that talk, I was charged in my spirit. I had had enough of this back and forth.

The surrender

Immediately, I began a fast. It was around 11:30pm on April 10th, 2023, when I stepped into the Throne Room of God. Yes, I had been praying for years about this matter but for the first time, I was ready to surrender to God's will.

All along, whenever I prayed for God to lead me in His will, I didn't mean it with all my heart. I didn't know this until I committed myself to prayer on that day. There was a complete death that had taken place, and I didn't care about what the answer would be. I was ready and willing to move right if God said right and left if He said left. And if He didn't say anything, I was prepared to knock and press on until I got an answer.

I realized that maybe God had been speaking all these years, perhaps even from the first day, but I was not hearing because it was not what I wanted to hear. That's what we often do to God. He may be speaking clearly but we sift His promptings, instructions, and directions to fit what we want. So, we analyze and analyze His instructions and ask for more and more signs because we wished He was saying something different. Then we create a complex situation for ourselves which the enemy takes advantage of to steal our peace. But all that was about to end. I was angry that I had fallen victim to the enemy's manipulation due to my own doubts and lack of conviction. I was angry that I had hurt Afriyie due to my own indecisiveness and ignorance. Now, I was ready to grow up and partner with God to bring

His perfect will to pass.

I prayed! I poured out my heart and I meant every word. The next day, April 11th, I continued to fast. I asked the Holy Spirit to lead me to the Word for the season and He graciously led me to the book of Esther. I wondered what the Lord had in store for me. The Holy Spirit instructed me to study the whole book of Esther, with emphasis on God and not Esther.

I had studied the book of Esther so many times and gleaned from the lives of the characters. One invisible Character we often gloss over is God. This time around, God was the main Character. I saw how God worked out His purpose to preserve a remnant of His people through Esther, Mordecai, the eunuchs, the officials and even Haman the enemy. The Holy Spirit showed me how God was in everything that happened, even taking advantage of Haman's wickedness to bring His people out of hiding and give them the opportunity to stand up for themselves against their enemies.

That evening, after work, I prayed earnestly, asking the Lord to work out His purpose for me and take advantage of the enemy's wickedness to lead His people to glory. I prayed about my path in life and asked the Lord to work things out so that equilibrium is ensured. I asked the Lord to take control of all things concerning me and lead me in the way He knew was right.

Day two came, and I was led to Nehemiah. Once again, the main Character under study was God. I saw God in action working things out, amid staunch opposition, to bring His divine purpose to pass. That evening, I prayed asking for the same things.

"Lord, lead me in the path you've chosen for me. I surrender to Your perfect will".

Day three was Ezra. A similar story to Nehemiah, and once again, God was assuring me of His ability to orchestrate His divine purpose for me irrespective of how unrelated the different parts may seem. He strengthened me on the inside and encouraged me to trust Him with my life. He made me, invested in me, and was greatly interested in me. Gently, He took the steering wheel from my hand and whispered, "trust Me".

That third night, I had a dream:

It was a quiet afternoon, and I was home with my mum. Suddenly, a thief tried to break in. The thief was a thick-tall, strong man, and looked somewhere in his forties. When we saw the man, we shouted, and he ran away. But in my spirit, I knew the thief would return. So that night, I couldn't sleep very well. I was on the lookout, staring at the window. Suddenly, a hand passed through the window toward me. The same thief we had seen that afternoon passed through the window as though it was a spirit and came into the room. I started fighting him with all of my strength. I hit him as hard as I could. He came in with a suitcase full of spectacles. I poured the spectacles on the floor and started breaking them one after the other and threw the pieces in his face. I pushed him outside the room and threw more pieces into his face. Suddenly, he started climbing the wall and coming towards me. I tried to push him, but he didn't budge. I called out to my mum who was in the room with me to help me push the man out, but she didn't respond. The man kept trying to re-enter the room and I kept trying to push him out with all my strength. He was a very strong man.

Then I woke up and wrote down the dream. I understood the dream immediately. I understood what those plenty spectacles stood for. They were the source of my confusion - varying images, many pictures being presented each time, altering my understanding. This thought here, that there, sometimes so many thoughts at the same time. My head was always full. But now, the Lord had given me victory over the strong man messing with my head. For the first time in a long time, I had peace within me. There was a quietness in my head. I praised God. The Lord helped me understand that I had to pray for my mum to also have peace concerning my future, especially, my marriage, so that she could stand with me against the enemy. I felt so much healthier and was confident of the future. I knew God was with me.

I continued to pray,

"Lord, please give me clarity, especially concerning my marriage. I have an idea of what You want me to do and who You want me to do it with, but I am not yet convinced about it. I need You to direct my path according to Your

Word in Proverbs 3:5-6. Please help me to have a conviction concerning the path You have called me to tread. Help my mum to align with Your will. Do this Lord, for the sake of Your glory and the purpose You have called me to".

I prayed this daily with all my heart and on April 20th, 2023, the answer came to me.

I dreamt and saw my traditional marriage ceremony. I wore a beautiful orange kente cloth and stood before my fathers who were presiding over the ceremony. They all commented on how beautiful I had grown to become, and they admired me greatly. I saw Pastor Afriyie Mensah, the groom, wearing a cream kaftan and also standing before my fathers. I was happy and satisfied. Everyone was so joyful. Then the setting changed, and I was standing with my mum in front of my apartment in the Western Region. She held out two cloths to me and asked for my opinion on which one to wear on my wedding day. I picked one of them and suddenly, she was wearing that cloth as a beautifully styled dress. She moved around so happily. She couldn't wait to wear it on my wedding day. As we stood in front of my door, I saw the optician at our eye care facility pass by. He looked me in the eyes and smiled at me. In the dream, I called my wedding, "The Pastors' Wedding".

I woke up with joy in my heart. The Holy Spirit appearing as an Optician in my dream meant that He had fixed the lenses I was seeing through. I could see better now. I knew it then but now, I was sure. I wrote down the dream and praised God.

Even though I had had this dream concerning my marital destiny, I didn't take any major step. I didn't call Afriyie or tell anyone about it. I wanted the Lord to orchestrate the remainder of what He had begun. I prayed to God to help Afriyie understand my path on earth so that he would stand by me, to my right, as a pillar of great support, as the Lord had shown me in a dream. I was concerned about some opinions Afriyie had expressed in the past about my academic path, so I asked the Lord to give him understanding. Though I was seeing him in my dreams and all, I needed to know that this man was compatible with me when it came to my purpose. It was a very important factor. The Lord had taught me this wisdom through the spiritual fathers and mothers I learned from. So, I stated my case before God:

"Abba, I have prayed to You and received this information in my dreams. But I need to also know for sure that Afriyie would not be a hindrance to the purpose you have called me to. He doesn't seem to understand why you are leading me on an academic path. Your daughter will only accept this man if he receives the right understanding to support me in the purpose you have called me to".

Purpose was and is extremely important to me. Purpose is the path cut out for me by God, and anything which stood against my purpose could not be the will of God for me.

For ten days, I said nothing to anyone. I had prayed to the Lord to cause Afriyie to contact me when the Lord had fixed his understanding. Otherwise, I would not budge.

1st May 2023, I received a call from Mrs. Ethel Zoe Koomson. She had been praying and the Holy Spirit led her to call me and inquire of the prayer assignment she gave me. I told her that I had received a message which indicated that Afriyie was the perfect will of God for me in marriage. I could sense the joy in her voice. She is such a completely beautiful woman. I, however, discussed with her the concerns I had. I felt Afriyie was not too excited about my intention to pursue a PhD. She assured me that she would relay my concerns to Afriyie and get back to me. I knew that God was working it out. Now I waited for Afriyie to contact me, according to the request I made of my God.

2nd May 2023, I received two e-books from Afriyie. They were *"Disciplines of a Godly Family"* by R. Kent Hughes and *"Disciplines of a Godly Woman"* by Barbara Hughes. He added, "Felt you would appreciate them! Blessings". I thanked him but didn't say anything else.

3rd May 2023, around 10:30am, I was praying in my consulting room when I received a much-awaited call. "Pastor Mensah" popped up on my phone and I was quick to answer. The mood was slightly tensed; the good kind of tensed…haha. He mentioned that he simply called to check up on me. We spoke for a few minutes, about nothing in particular, but we both understood very well what was happening between us. We knew too well what had just begun between us. At the end of the conversation, we could not tell each other what we really wanted to say. I wanted to tell Afriyie that I appreciated his resilience all these years and I loved him…I really did. For the first time, I allowed myself to love him as a woman loves a man. I wondered if it was too early to tell him. About a minute after we ended the call, I got a message from him which read, "I love you, my girl! Be safe!" I felt really warm. Afriyie had loved me for years and I had never reciprocated it. I felt quite sorry but also hopeful because I still had the chance to love him as much as he should be loved. I responded, "I love you too, my man!" He sent me a smiling face emoji.

That evening, we spoke at length on the phone. I told him that I had accepted a PhD offer and was pursuing a career in academia. I knew he had heard it from Mrs. Koomson, but I wanted to hear his response for myself.

Afriyie's ardent support of my academic journey began that evening. He was incredibly excited and throughout my journey to this day, has been my number one fan. It turns out what I interpreted as apathy concerning this path was his worry about delayed marriage to a woman who was about to embark on a five-year PhD journey.

And it was on! A&A (Afriyie & Asantewaa), love birds divinely joined, divinely helped, and divinely sustained.

CHAPTER FIVE: A&A

It had been a long way coming. For Afriyie, his journey could be summed up in two words - patience and perseverance. For me, I would say, prayerfulness and dying to self. For both of us, it had been a journey of God's mercy.

Though I was adamant to the promptings of the Holy Spirit at first, there was a gradual progression in my willingness to lay my will aside and wholly follow the path the Lord was leading me on. There was a gradual death and by the time the Holy Spirit had finished His work in me regarding this matter, I had become His partner in purpose, through prayer and obedience, to establish His perfect plan for me and indirectly, for many others whose destinies were connected to my obedience.

I was glad the Lord did not shove me into an "arranged marriage" I did not understand but took time to help me become a person with the right perspective of who God is and why His perfect will mattered most. It was indisputable that the Lord wanted Afriyie and me together. I did not know all the details concerning this plan, but I was willing to take a step into the unknown, trusting that God knew the way. Most importantly, I was one with God on this, His agenda had become my agenda, and I willingly held His hand to bring it to pass.

There was an unusual peace in my spirit. I was so happy that God had been patient with me all these years and helped me to accept His will for me. For the next few days, I could not make any requests of God for myself. I simply thanked Him. For some reason unknown to me, my heart was filled with joy.

The first days of A&A were a catching up period. I was curious to know more about him and what he had been up to, and he also had a lot of questions. We had long conversations deep into the night and prayed together as often as we could.

A few days into it and I realized something unfavorable about my man. Afriyie was not as spiritually sound as I had known him to be some years ago. He was no longer the very enthusiastic evangelist I met three years ago. Other things seemed to occupy most of his time. He was still a Christian, a good one, but not as "hot" as he used to be.

I took the matter to God and it became a prayer point and assignment. I began to understand why the Lord brought me into his life at that time. We talked about it and he acknowledged and expressed concern about it. We asked for the help of the Holy Spirit and began our journey to a revival. I saw it as a project the Lord had entrusted to me. In fact, the moment A&A began, everything about Afriyie was of great concern to me. I prayed for him even much more than I prayed for myself. And thankfully, Afriyie was humble to acknowledge the unhealthy state of his spiritual life and accept help.

We prayed every chance we got. We scheduled a midnight prayer date and prayed! After praying, we chatted for another hour or two, and when the time to say goodbye came, we just kept talking because none of us could end the call. It was a mixture of spiritual awakening and feelings awakening. I was excited to see Afriyie's progress over time and it was wonderful to witness how much God doted on him and valued his destiny. I was very happy to partner with God to help His son.

I wanted to do well in this courtship and eventually in our marriage, so I prayed for wisdom. I had read some books and listened to a lot of messages on marriage and courtship but here I was experiencing it firsthand, and I really didn't want to mess things up. When I asked for wisdom, the Holy Spirit took me to James 3:17,

"But the wisdom that is from above is first pure, then peaceful, gentle, reasonable, full of mercy and good fruits, without partiality, and without hypocrisy."

I meditated on this scripture and made it my guide. I found obedience to this scripture to characterize the life of a wise person. It is wise to be peace-loving and gentle. It is wise to be submissive and easy to reason with. It is wise to be impartial, exhibiting mercy and good fruits. It was a guide for every relationship or partnership. In all my ways, I purposed to follow this scripture. I knew it was not going to be all rosy and mushy all the time, but I could help keep things peaceful and loving by adhering to the guidelines in this scripture. I shared this with Afriyie, and it became our scripture.

All was going well. I met some of his friends over the phone and they were all very lovely and kind. One thing I loved so much was the kind of people he had around him. His people were God-people, the kind Christ described as His mother, sister and brother in Matthew 12:48-50. It made it easy to fit in.

I still had a few doubts here and there. Afriyie and I had known each other mainly over the phone. We had met in person only a few times. Hm. I wondered if we would be sexually compatible. What were his opinions on this very very important topic? I wondered about a lot of things in that area and asked God a few "innocent" questions. It's important, you know?

About two weeks later, Pastor Charles informed me that he had come to the Western Region of Ghana where I was working. I was happy to hear that but was also a little sad that Afriyie did not come along. I longed to see him. I called Afriyie and he mentioned that he was in another part of Ghana for some business. How I wished he came along.

In the afternoon, around 4pm, Pastor Charles passed by the clinic to pay me a visit. After exchanging pleasantries, he mentioned that Afriyie gave him a gift to give to me which was in the trunk of his car. He opened the trunk and to my greatest surprise, the best gift I could receive that day…Afriyie himself all giggly as they laughed at the shock on my face.

He gave me a little hug and I just couldn't believe that he was right there in front of me. Pastor Charles took leave of us for some personal business and A&A were left alone. We went to the mall and had dinner. The mood was a bit tensed, like two teenagers who had liked each other from afar and were meeting face-to-face for the first time. For hours, we talked about our journey and how we felt at that moment.

Afriyie was more expressive with his feelings, not just verbally but he expressed it even in how he held my hands. He looked at me like a man looks at a woman he loves. Those hours together were Heaven's answer to the doubts I was having. The attraction was there. Sparks flew and so did the butterflies in my tummy whenever he was inches away. We both knew it, and it was settled.

Sex before marriage or any form of sexual immorality was off the table and an absolute no. But I was glad that the attraction was present because as I said earlier, it is very very important.

A lot of things were unfolding, and I wished I could share them with my mum. She had been my closest friend for years and I didn't want to hide these wonderful moments from her. But I couldn't share these with her because I knew her stance concerning Afriyie and me. She had never been in support, but I needed her blessing now. This was God-ordained, and I needed my mum to be a part of it.

In that season, I came across a video of another wonderful woman of God (Pastor KK) in which she shared her journey toward marriage. Like my situation, her mother was also not in support of her choice of a marital partner. Pastor KK described how The Holy Spirit guided her to pray for her mother and against any manipulating spirit behind her mother's disposition. Listening to her, I realized that my mum was not viciously trying to hinder God's purpose for me. She needed help, just like I did, to come into agreement with God. So instead of fighting her or arguing unnecessarily, Afriyie and I prayed for her with all our hearts.

One Saturday, I was home with my mum chatting about random things. Then from nowhere, unintentionally, we began to talk about marriage. As we spoke, I prayed within, "Lord, please give me an opening". Slowly, I brought the issue up. I told my mum all that had happened in the past few weeks, my journey to the conviction I held onto so strongly, who I had known Afriyie to be, and the growth A&A had experienced in such a short time.

I didn't have to talk much. It seemed that my mum had been picking some signals in my speech and behavior those past weeks. She simply asked me one question, "do you love him?" I responded, "of course, I do". She looked at me so warmly and with so much concern, as if to ask, "are you sure about this?" I told her that I had trusted God all my life and He had never failed once. It was a journey of faith and God was in this.

CHAPTER FIVE: A&A

A few days later, Afriyie sent me a screenshot of a message he had received from a "stranger". It was a very encouraging message.

Afriyie wondered if it could really be my mum sending him such a message and why. I asked my mum about it, and she told me that she chanced upon the quote somewhere and just felt like encouraging Afriyie. I was shocked!

Afriyie's experiences with my mum had been terrible. But now, my mum was reaching out, as though she was putting out her hand for a reconciliatory handshake. Though she didn't say it out loud, I knew my mum was carrying a burden of guilt. She regretted her treatment of Afriyie but just didn't know how to apologize or reconcile with him. By reaching out first, she made her intentions known and it was easy for Afriyie to also reach out to her. I respect my mum so much for her humility and willingness to join hands with us. God was with us every step of the way. Before I prayed, He had answered.

I was loving who Afriyie was. His spiritual life was healing, and I was so glad to be a part of the process.

His finances were however down. Certain investments had gone wrong, some businesses were not picking up as fast as desired, he was emotionally down sometimes, and once again, I praised God for bringing me in at that time of his life to exhort his spirit, contribute ideas, and hold his hands in prayer.

He shared his day-to-day affairs with me, all the ups and downs. I encouraged, constructively criticized when needed, and made sure that he went to bed with less burdens. The Lord had taught me well over the years and I applied James 3:17 in all situations. To be very honest, I was happy to be part of Afriyie's rocky moments. I learned his moods and vulnerabilities. I learned when to speak and when to just be quiet. And when I spoke, I spoke with carefulness and the wisdom James 3:17 had taught me.

We continued to pray in the night. Every midnight, we had a prayer date over the phone. We poured out our hearts to God, praised and worshipped our Lord, and then talked about life. Those night talks pulled us closer to each other.

The more I got to know Afriyie, the more I

understood why the Lord put us together. Our personalities were completely different- he was like a hot sunny afternoon, filled with festivities and street carnivals, hot spicy food, loud music and bright warm colors, and I was like a lakeside book review meeting at sunset, with the birds chirping in the background and the cool breeze blowing against our light blankets. He liked pictures and fashion and all that, and I, well, liked none of those. I was a good book on a Sunday afternoon, no disturbances kind of girl. But when we came together, we didn't clash. We simply blended and balanced each other. He brought me out of my shell, and I cooled him down a bit.

It was not logical the way we blended so well. From afar, I thought he would be shy, but he was the complete opposite. He was not shy at all; he was expressive and charming. He had his flaws, but he accepted correction so readily that it was easy to help him. He was not perfect, and his imperfections became my ministry in his life.

Though our personalities were very different, our core nature was strangely the same. We didn't grow up together or know each other before then but whenever we talked, we found that we had very similar dreams and hopes. When it came to the things that mattered, we shared very similar opinions. Our vision board looked almost the same, the burdens in our hearts were the same, we shared similar gifts of writing and teaching, we were evangelists by calling, philanthropy held a very high position in our hearts... we simply spoke the same language when it came to ministry and the Kingdom of our God. It was baffling how two very different personalities could be so similar in another facet. Only God could establish such a union. To the logical mind, A&A made no sense, but to God, we were the perfect pair for His work.

Most importantly, God was with us. God was interested in us. This union was not just about two individuals coming together as husband and wife; there was a bigger agenda which was not fully known to us. It felt like going on an adventure, holding tightly onto the promise of God to be with me throughout the journey. I had partnered with God to bring His grand mysterious agenda to pass.

Did we have disagreements in the dating process? Yes! Did we upset each other at times? Yes! Did we struggle with natural sexual urges? A big YES! The normal things happened to us but our responses to those things were guided by the Holy Spirit in us and not our flesh. There was always that still small voice that kept us from straying.

During those early days of our relationship, God spoke severally to me through dreams. Most of those messages were warnings about things we should pay attention to, especially in prayer. God revealed the agenda of the enemy against this union and urged us to pray. Why was God revealing these only to me? In that season, I understood my role as the "gate" and "heart" of the union. I was the channel of spiritual information, and I passed it on to Afriyie, who eagerly joined me in prayer. We were only a few weeks into the relationship but obviously, God had been working on this a long time because the progress was simply incredible.

July was fast approaching. I was about entering a new phase of my life. Academia was my "courtyard"- a seemingly non-religious altar upon which I gave God the returns for the academic grace He invested in me. I was excited about starting my PhD in Vision Science. A part of me was also a bit sad because I would be miles away from my family and my Afriyie. All-in-all, we were full of joy; our

God had been faithful to us.

Preparations for my upcoming travel began. I knew it was going to be very cost intensive, considering the plane ticket cost, visa application fee etc., and money for general upkeep for my first month of stay in the US, among other things. There was also a tall list of things I needed to buy before travelling. Counting the cost, I knew that I couldn't afford 10% of the things I needed. So, I did what I knew to do best - pray. God gave me an instruction in that season to write down everything I thought I would need for the journey. I did. He gave me a Scripture:

'For Yahweh says, "You will not see wind, neither will you see rain, yet that valley will be filled with water, and you will drink, both you and your livestock and your other animals. This is an easy thing in Yahweh's sight." ' (2 Kings 3:17-18a)

By this Word, I was encouraged. I sowed a seed of thanksgiving and continued praying. The first miracle came on the first day of April. By the Hand of God, an amount of money which had to be refunded to me due to a cancelled purchase, and which I had long been waiting for, finally hit my account. I was so happy that I cried. I added to it and paid my visa appointment fee. Not long after that, God gave me great favor in the eyes of my boss, Dr. Jerome Abaka-Cann, who, together with his wonderful wife, paid my SEVIS fee (a necessity for my visa interview and entry into the US as a student). Things were happening. The valley was miraculously filling with water.

When Afriyie came in, both my visa and SEVIS fees had been paid. But the main chunk of the cost was still not covered. I needed a plane ticket and just checking prices online made me anxious. The dollar-cedi exchange rate had skyrocketed and I needed at least USD1,250 for a one-way economy-class ticket with at least two stops. Both Afriyie and I didn't have that money. My family didn't have it either. So, myself, my mum and Afriyie called out to the God who fills valleys with supernatural water. We prayed.

One dawn, as Afriyie and I were praying over the phone concerning this matter, he burst into tears. The matter had become his matter. He prayed as one prays fervently for oneself. I was moved and secretly, I thanked God for such a man.

On July 15, Pastor Charles Koomson and Afriyie Mensah came to Takoradi, where I lived, for a friend's wedding. After the event, we took a long road trip to Accra, the capital city of Ghana, where the Koomsons lived. This also was an answered prayer because I needed a place to lodge in Accra for my visa interview which would take place on the 20th of July. God was killing many birds with one stone. I was so happy to meet Mummy Ethel Koomson in person for the first time. It was such a wonderful moment. I was also very excited to see Afriyie in person. We talked for hours; to each other and to God. For six days, we stayed with the Koomsons. I particularly enjoyed the early morning Bible studies and the long rides through the city. All of it was very refreshing.

One of those evenings, Afriyie knocked on my door. We had been praying all that while, but that evening was quite different. We knelt, held hands and prayed. We prayed! During the prayer, I had a knowing that I should call a certain man and ask for his help with the ticket. I brushed that "feeling" aside and continued to pray. After praying, that nudge was still there. I excused myself, went to the washroom and discussed what I was sensing with

God. I told the Lord that I did not want to rely on my own understanding so if that direction was not from Him, He should keep me from taking any wrong step. I returned to Afriyie, and we talked for hours as though tomorrow would not come.

The next day, I still felt that nudge. So, I prayed again, picked my phone, and called Dr. Kwaku Osei. This wonderful man had been so helpful in my preparation towards my graduate school interview. When I called him, it was difficult for me to bring up the issue at hand, but God gave me courage. I told him that I needed help in buying a ticket for my flight. He replied eagerly that he had been wondering about how I was faring financially because he had been in my shoes some years ago and knew that it was not so easy to gather funds in such times. He simply told me to relax and focus on my upcoming interview. About two hours later, he inquired about a few demographic details. By midday, a ticket landed in my inbox. I was beyond happy. I cried out in joy, informed everyone around me and called my mum and Dr. Abaka-Cann to inform them of what God had just done for me. I couldn't thank Dr. Osei enough. I just kept going on and on. He replied that he simply wanted to be part of my journey. I don't know about you but that was favor in every sense of the word.

The plane ticket was settled and now the visa interview was next. Thursday, July 20th 2023, Pastor Charles, Afriyie and I arose at dawn and set out for the embassy. We sang along the way and got there about 3 hours early. My interview was another experience of great favor, and my visa application was approved. Our hearts were glad indeed.

I was happy that everything had fallen in place and even more glad that there were genuine people around to celebrate with me.

The next day, Afriyie and I travelled to Kumasi. I met his family, friends, and spiritual leaders. Honestly, I felt like a princess. Everyone was eagerly looking forward to meeting me and they were all so kind and accepting. I left for Cape Coast and told my mum about everything I had experienced.

July 28th, my mum and I travelled to Accra and lodged at the Koomsons'. Afriyie was also there. That evening, Afriyie and I had a long chat. I knew it was quite difficult for him that soon, I would be so far from him. The next day, we left for the airport, said our goodbyes, and I was up in the sky, on my way to a new land, eagerly anticipating what God had in store for me.

CHAPTER SIX: MILES APART

Twenty hours later, I stepped onto American soil. The good Lord had prepared helpers for me and I settled in so effortlessly. The PhD was on.

Afriyie and I had spent most of our relationship miles apart, with him being in the middle belt of Ghana and me at the south. We mostly spoke over the phone and so I did not think that being in different countries would impact our relationship in any way. I was wrong.

My days as a graduate student were packed. 24 hours never seemed enough. I had so much on my to-do list and Afriyie was often not on that list. We could go days without talking. He knew that I had a busy schedule and so he didn't complain much but it was clear that he was not happy with the situation. I realized that if our communication would not suffer, I had to be intentional about it. Many times, we tried without success to schedule a date where we could catch up, pray, and plan our future.

In the early weeks of 2024, I began to have doubts concerning A&A. I questioned the decision I had taken to be with Afriyie. It was almost as though I was not the same person who had emerged from the Throne Room with a conviction. There was a battle in my mind. Had I made the right decision? What if Afriyie changed and became a monster I couldn't recognize? What if I met someone better? A part of me felt that I could give myself space to explore more options. Where were these thoughts coming from?

It is not unusual to wonder whether one's choice of a life-partner is a good enough decision. Marriage is a huge deal after all. But the battle going on inside me was too intense. I couldn't break free from these overpowering thoughts, and I began to assess Afriyie all over again and his flaws stood out to me. They were so magnified in my mind that I became anxious of the future.

Was it because he had experienced major financial losses and was thrown into a quagmire, almost without any clear direction for the future? Was I interpreting this as a sign that he had lost his bearing and could not lead me? Was I anxious of what the future held for me as Mrs. Afriyie Mensah? A few times, I imagined myself calling Afriyie and saying the words, "I can't do this with you anymore, I'm out".

But why? A few months ago, I was sure. What was happening to my conviction? Maybe, the anxiety in my heart could be explained by the circumstances in that season, but I had experienced a bit of the devil's tactics in the past and the situation looked like a good substrate to grow confusion, fear and eventually, a break-up.

About that time, Pastor Charles reached out to me with a message. It was so strange because we had not had any major conversation since I left for the US. Interestingly, the message hit the nail right on the head.

That call from Pastor Charles woke me up from my long slumber. I called Afriyie that day and we spoke at length. For the first time in a long while, we planned a prayer schedule and decided to be more intentional about communicating frequently. I was honest with Afriyie. I told him everything that was going on in my mind and the call I had received from Pastor Charles which confirmed what I had been experiencing. We decided that the season of coldness and prayerlessness had to end. There was a viper hiding in the wood and only fire could expose it. We began to pray.

For a while, I had not prayed with Afriyie and so I was completely unaware of the spiritual rehabilitation the Lord had taken him through. There was a fire, that fire which I perceived in the early days of our encounter about four years prior. It had dwindled, even to the point of making me anxious about his spiritual health. I had been praying about it, asking the Lord to renew that burning zeal. It had been about six months since we prayed seriously together, and I was pleasantly surprised. During our prayer, I would stop and simply listen to him pray with so much passion. I would thank God in my heart for this revival in Afriyie that I was witnessing. I would admire Afriyie and smile to myself, because there was nothing I desired more in a man than one who loved and feared the Lord with all his heart.

During one of our conversations, he excitedly briefed me on an evangelism he had embarked on that day. Truth be told, it had been a while since I heard him talk so enthusiastically about evangelism. He had succeeded in converting an unbeliever, whom he met in a public transport bus, to Christianity. He told me how he had missed preaching the Gospel in buses and taxis, something he used to do very often when he did not have a car. Financially, things were down. Spiritually, things had never been so up. Afriyie was returning to his well. I did not have all the answers to what was going on in his life, but I was absolutely sure that God was with him. It gave me peace.

The reigniting of our prayer altar also reignited our passion for each other. I had missed him so much. We spoke for hours whenever we had the chance and maybe for the very first time, started to make serious plans toward our wedding and our life together.

Around that same time, I was in the middle of publishing my first book, *"My Old Friend with No Name"*. About ten months prior, I had spoken to Afriyie about my desire to publish a book The Holy Spirit had inspired me to write. He advised that I hold on and pray about it until the season was right. In January 2024, I had a knowing in my heart that it was time. I read through the manuscript and prepared it for publication. I had no idea how it would get published, how I would fund the process or even the publishing firm to submit the manuscript to. All I knew was that it was time, and God would work it out. And indeed, He did.

In February 2024, I joined an online prayer session hosted by Pastor JJ. The woman of God led us to pray for helpers who had the right information, the right interpretation, and could support the execution of our dreams. I prayed those prayers with tears in my eyes. I needed help to realize my dream of becoming a published author.

In that same February, I chanced upon an advertisement on Instagram. A thriving Christian publishing firm was soliciting manuscripts for publication. My heart leaped within me. I prayed to God for guidance and in two days, I submitted the manuscript to the company. I received an email from them, and I was en route to becoming an author. When preparation meets a divinely orchestrated opportunity, success is inevitable.

Of course, I shared the news with Afriyie, and we dedicated time to praying about the publication process, the release of the book and its impact on humanity.

In that season, I felt an urgent need for Afriyie to seriously seek the Face of God concerning his purpose and future. It was not as though he didn't know his purpose, but I felt that God had something new for him and was waiting for him in the secret place. I had shared this with him at the beginning of the year, but it took some time for him to do so.

In the early days of April, he travelled to a solitary place to spend time with God. As was his custom, he turned off his phone, put everything on hold and went on a retreat. My excitement was through the roof. I knew within me that God had something very special for him and the time Afriyie would spend alone with God would be as those days when Moses ascended the mountain of God, dwelt in God's presence, and came down with a glowing face. Seven days later, we spoke on the phone. I was curious to know how his time with God went.

The Afriyie that came back from that retreat was set loose and ready to soar. He admitted to me that prior to that retreat, he always felt a hindrance whenever he wanted to pray or evangelize. It was not as though he didn't want to, but he always had to force himself to do them. The conflict between his spirit and his flesh was too strong.

God helped him break free. He told me, "I did not have a supernatural encounter or an angelic visitation during the retreat, but God dealt with me on many levels". I was pleased to hear that because many of us judge the effectiveness of prayer or a spiritual exercise by supernatural manifestations. Many times, it is the heart that receives a makeover and is enlightened by God's Word during that process. This renewing and illumination, in turn, can change everything.

The Afriyie that came back seven days later had a new drive and I prayed it wouldn't dwindle. With that drive, he revamped "Zionytes World Outreach", an intercessory and evangelistic ministry with the goal of proclaiming the Gospel to all and sundry, and preparing the hearts of men toward the second coming of our Lord Jesus Christ.

I knew that God had sent me to Afriyie as a prophet and spiritual helper. Sometimes, however, I was inappropriate in my approach to helping him find God's purpose for him in a certain season. Unconsciously, I was developing an overbearing and authoritative stance which made him defensive on some occasions. To me, I was simply trying to help him by partnering with God concerning his destiny but unconsciously, I was trying to be his God. I was trying to fix him and have him where I thought God wanted him. My general motive was good, but underlying it was a growing domineering attitude. The Holy Spirit nipped it in the bud before it became an inferno of pride.

It was in that season that I encountered a teaching on YouTube by Pastor Debola Deji-Kurunmi, popularly known as DDK.

Have you ever listened to a teaching and felt immediately that it was prepared with you in mind? Whenever I listened to a teaching by DDK, 2 Timothy 3:16-17 came alive.

"Every Scripture is God-breathed and profitable for

teaching, for reproof, for correction, and for instruction in righteousness, that each person who belongs to God may be complete, thoroughly equipped for every good work."

I felt the loving but stern rebuke of God. I felt enlightened in a very strange way as though I was seeing for the first time; the Word of God came alive in me! DDK would say, "God told me to tell His daughters...", and I would sit up and listen with rapt attention because I felt the message was directly for me. God used DDK to correct some wrong perspectives I had concerning a woman's role in marriage, and to teach me the agenda God had in mind for His daughters in this era. I saw a brave and powerful woman who at the same time was gentle and submissive to God and her husband. God gifted me a role model.

The illumination I obtained revealed the fault in my thinking and the subtle domineering attitude I was developing over Afriyie. You see, sometimes the desire to fix people and rule over them can shroud itself in a cloak of false humility and "good" intentions. I loved Afriyie and wanted him to do well. But instead of approaching him as a submissive helpmeet, unconsciously, I was playing the role of a mother trying to straighten her ten-year old son.

And because Afriyie is a grown man and not a ten-year old boy, it is expected that he would resist the invasion into his autonomy, which is exactly what he did.

"I am not his lord; I am his helper. I am not his lord; I am his helper". It became my song. My duty was to respectfully, carefully and prayerfully guide and help him, not to be his lord.

The resistance of my flesh to the will of God did not cease immediately. My flesh didn't agree with God at all, but I was adamant to heeding its protests. My spirit wanted to align with God's agenda, though there was still work to be done for a complete alignment.

Whenever the enemy brought up all the reasons why Afriyie was not "good enough", my spirit did not completely resist him. A part of me wanted to side with my flesh. And because the agreement between my spirit and God was not complete, it was easy for negative thoughts to thrive in my mind. I was tolerating the enemy because the greater part of me was still against God's will. I had given the enemy a resting place in my mind.

For anyone who desires to do the will of God, the

stance of your spirit cannot be divided between God and your flesh. A complete agreement with God is needed. Your flesh might be weak, but your spirit must be completely willing to do God's will. This gives room for the Holy Spirit to intervene. You cannot fight what you are consciously or unconsciously in agreement with.

This light came to me on the 26th of September 2024. I listened to a message by an amazing woman of God (Pastor BB) on the topic of demonic influences. I had been praying concerning the negative seeds being sown in my mind and God showed me the underlying cause. I had to break that agreement with the enemy that was against my marriage. I had to resist the enemy. Only then would he flee.

With that light, I declared my position, "I am with God, I submit to His will, and I resist the enemy". Then, I asked the Holy Spirit to help my flesh.

So many times, the enemy showed up with new tricks. The more I realized how much the enemy did not want my marriage to Afriyie to stand, the more resilient I became in my spirit and in the place of prayer. Whatever it was that the kingdom of darkness was so afraid of, I wanted to birth it, and no dragon could devour it because it was drenched in the Blood of Jesus!

CHAPTER SEVEN: THE PASTORS' WEDDING

I am writing this chapter on the 6th of March 2025. As I sit here about to document this part, I am almost in disbelief seeing how far God has brought me. Afriyie and I have chosen May 31st, 2025, as the day we tie the knot. What a journey this has been!

Just a few days ago, Pastor Charles finalized the foreword for this book. The Koomsons and I have planned the perfect wedding gift and surprise for Afriyie. He has no idea that I have been writing about our journey. This book is my gift to my husband. I look forward to the shock on his face when I give him the first copy on May 31st, 2025.

It is amazing how God works. Five years ago, on March 6th, 2020, I had no idea that I was chosen to pass through the valley, glean such timeless lessons, and share them with you. I didn't know that I would meet an Afriyie and through that one man, God would fix my heart and make me a blessing. I didn't know that my marriage was anointed to be a loud and powerful message to all of God's people. In my light, many will see light.

Preparations are underway. I am excited and nervous at the same time. As for Afriyie, he is over the moon.

CHAPTER EIGHT: I WRITE TO YOU, DEAR CHILD OF GOD

The distractors are many. Many things compete for your attention but only one deserves to have it. And that all-important thing is "what is God saying?". This can be put in other ways: "what is God seeing?", "what is God's will in this matter?", "what is most important to God in this matter?". Do you see that the value of a thing is directly linked to what God thinks of it? Every man or woman derives their substance from what God makes of them. This is the most important factor in choosing a marital partner. Anything that clutters your attention to what God is saying is a distractor.

When I met Afriyie, I knew in my heart that God

considered him perfect for me. But the distractors were many. For three years, God, by His mercy and love for me, opened my eyes to see beyond the glaring attention-grabbers and perceive what He sees in Afriyie. God did not remove the distractors, rather, He helped me to see beyond them and understand just how insignificant they are compared to the substance of a person.

I understand that it can be very difficult, almost heart wrenching, to let go of your idea of a perfect spouse to accept God's will for you. It takes a lot of strength to surrender. The distractors scream but God nudges your heart ever so mildly and whispers, "trust Me".

For a child who loves their Father, that little nudge can feel like a sharp sword piercing one's heart. It unsettles you. It breaks your heart because you love Him. You want to follow the path He's hinting at, but your will is strong and the attention-grabbers make it very difficult. I understand you. God made me pass through it and experience every heart-wrenching moment of surrendering to His will so that I can say and mean the words, "I understand how you feel". But I also know by experiencing it that there is no greater peace than the peace that floods your heart when you know that you allowed God, your good and merciful Father, to have His way.

You need strength to obey God against your will. That strength is the Holy Spirit. When you feel overwhelmed, confused and tired, remember that the Spirit of God is in you to help and strengthen you. He is indispensable to your letting go and allowing God.

Dear daughter of the King, you are loved by your Father in Heaven. You are valuable to Him. For you, He has a perfect plan. He earnestly searches the hearts of men and chooses a type of man most suitable for the fulfilment of your glorious purpose on earth. You have the power to choose your spouse based on what you desire in a husband but always remember that as a daughter of God, you have the advantage of knowing the perfect will of God and receiving strength from His Spirit to follow that will. You have a great advantage to know the mind of an infinitely loving God concerning your marital destiny.

Dear son of the King, you are a valiant prince of the Kingdom of God. Your divine mandate is priceless. For you, God has made a suitable helper. He made you and knows what complements your makeup. You can choose your spouse in accordance with your desires but first remember that your All-knowing Father has an opinion concerning your marital destiny. He wants a word with you.

What do you say? Will you listen to what God is saying? Will you partner with Him to establish His Kingdom through your marriage?

The end.

ABOUT THE AUTHOR

Dr. Asantewaa Aboagye-MacCarthy is a writer, an award-winning author and a dedicated teacher of God's Word. She serves as the president of Goshen Family, a philanthropic youth organization committed to making a positive impact. Professionally, she is an optometrist and is currently pursuing a PhD in vision science. When she's not in the lab, she enjoys journaling and watching medieval movies with friends.

Other books by the author

My Old Friend with No Name

When You Decide to Break Free

The Word by a God-Girl for a God-Girl

Daughter of the King, Pray

www.ingramcontent.com/pod-product-compliance
Lightning Source LLC
Chambersburg PA
CBHW070507100426
42743CB00010B/1783